Printed in the USA
CPSIA information can be obtained
at www.ICGtesting.com
LVHW081701210923
758946LV00013B/420

9 781690 725824